Chapter 1: Concrete Dreams

The court was cracked.

The net was torn.

The backboard leaned like it was tired of holding dreams.

But to Jamari?

That half-court slab of concrete behind the apartments might as well have been Madison Square Garden.

It was where he first learned to dribble — using a ball with barely any grip.

Where he shot jumpers into the wind with both hands like a slingshot.

Where he told himself, over and over,

"I'ma make the league one day."

No one believed him. Not really.

His mother worked double shifts and barely had time to come to games.

The boys on the block laughed when he said he'd be the first out.

His real father dipped before he could walk.

The only one around was his stepfather — Marcus.

Marcus didn't do the whole "pat you on the head" thing.

Didn't call Jamari "champ" or "killer" or any of the other names coaches threw around.

He just watched.

Studied.

Silently judged.

And when Jamari finally worked up the nerve to ask him what he thought of his game, Marcus didn't flinch.

"You good."

That was it.

Not "great." Not "next up."

Just good.

But the way Marcus said it… it didn't feel like a compliment. It felt like a challenge.

"You think I'm not working hard enough?" Jamari snapped one evening.

They were walking back from the rec. Jamari had just scored 28 in a summer league game. The crowd loved him. He thought that would be the night Marcus finally gave him some credit.

Marcus kept walking.

Didn't even look over his shoulder.

"You wanna be good? Keep doing what you're doing."

"You wanna be great?"

He paused.

"Then get ready to hate me."

That night, Jamari lay on his twin mattress, staring at the ceiling fan. Sweat still clung to his arms. His knees ached. His ego ached more.

Everyone else said he was nice.

The coaches said he had potential.

Kids in the stands called him "the truth."

But his own stepfather?

Acted like he was just okay.

The next morning, before the sun came up, Marcus stood in the doorway of Jamari's room.

"Up."

Jamari rubbed his eyes.

"For what?"

"You said you wanted this, right?"

He pointed to the scuffed-up basketball at the edge of the bed.

"Then let's see if you mean it."

They hit the court by 6:15 AM. No lights, just sunrise.

"Same move. Same footwork. Until I say stop," Marcus barked.

Jamari looked confused.

"That's it? No cones? No drills?"

Marcus smiled coldly.

"You wanna be flashy… or you wanna be unstoppable?"

By 7:00 AM, Jamari's shirt was soaked.

By 7:15, he was breathing like he ran a mile.

By 7:30, he hated the game.

"Again," Marcus said.

"Man, I already hit it like ten times!"

Marcus walked over, took the ball, and stared Jamari down.

"I don't count makes until you're tired.

Anybody can hoop fresh.

But when your legs burn… when your chest tight…

That's when it counts."

Jamari didn't respond. He just wiped his face, took the ball, and got back in position.

Somewhere between the twelfth and thirtieth rep, he stopped thinking.

Stopped talking.

Stopped trying to prove anything.

He just worked.

Chapter 2: Good Ain't Great

The gym smelled like sweat, rubber, and something that might've been fried chicken hours ago. A row of duffel bags lined the bleachers like sleeping soldiers. The hardwood gleamed under overhead lights, freshly waxed. You could hear sneakers squeaking before you even opened the doors.

This wasn't Jamari's usual spot.

This wasn't his boys from the neighborhood or his high school teammates.

This was the run — the one Marcus told him about but never brought him to.

Until today.

"What kind of gym is this?" Jamari asked as they walked in.

Marcus didn't answer right away. He nodded toward the court, where six players ran 5-on-5 with a kind of sharpness Jamari hadn't seen before.

"You'll see," Marcus finally said.

The runs were private. Invitation only.

But Marcus knew somebody, who knew somebody, and now Jamari was suiting up.

He looked around:

One kid had a Kansas warm-up shirt on. Another had bounced back from a prep school in Arizona. Two others were already committed to D1 programs. They didn't talk much. They didn't smile.

They just played.

And they played hard.

Jamari's first touch came off a kick-out. He pump-faked, took a dribble, rose up — and got swatted into the wall.

Nobody even helped him up.

One of the older guys laughed.

"That weak stuff don't fly here, rook."

Next possession, Jamari tried to go baseline. Cut off. Step-back jumper. Clank.

Then he got lost on a defensive switch.

Then picked at half-court.

By the third game, his shirt clung to him like wet plastic.

His hands were shaking. His confidence? Leaking out with every missed shot.

He caught Marcus watching from the corner of the gym — arms crossed, expression flat.

After the run, Jamari sat on the floor, head down.

His lungs burned. His pride? Gone.

"They different," he mumbled.

Marcus walked over and tossed him a towel.

"Nah," he said. "They just work harder than you. Longer than you. With more truth than you."

Jamari looked up, hurt.

"So you don't think I'm built for this?"

"I think," Marcus said, crouching beside him, "you believe in the version of yourself that ain't been tested yet."

He stood.

"You think you want the league — until the league shows you what it actually takes."

The ride home was silent.

Jamari stared out the window, replaying every turnover in his head.

Every time he froze.

Every moment he realized... he wasn't the best on the floor.

Maybe not even top five.

When they got back to the house, Marcus didn't say anything.

He just walked to the garage, opened the side door, and turned on the light.

The gym.

Weights. Jump ropes. A dusty treadmill. A full rack of basketballs.

"You got cooked," he said finally, not even turning around.

"That ain't shameful.

But what would be shameful is if you don't use it."

Jamari didn't respond.

He didn't have to.

He dropped his bag.

Laced up his shoes.

And walked inside.

Chapter 3: The Runback

The next morning, Jamari didn't wait for Marcus to knock.

He was already dressed. Shoes tied. Hoodie on.

Ball in his hand.

Marcus raised an eyebrow when he walked into the living room.

"You ready to work?" he asked.

Jamari didn't say a word.

He just nodded.

They hit the garage gym again.

But something was different.

There was no music. No small talk.

Just squeaking soles, deep breaths, and the thud of the ball against concrete.

"Same move. One thousand times," Marcus said, pointing to the cone.

Jamari nodded and got to work. Crossover. Jab. Pull-up.

Again.

And again.

After the first hour, sweat poured like rain.

By hour two, Jamari's arms felt like bricks.

His calves locked up.

He wanted to quit — but didn't.

"Why this move?" Jamari asked between gasps.

Marcus handed him a water bottle but didn't answer right away.

"Because it's the move you messed up most at the run," he finally said.

"The one that got you blocked. The one that made you second guess."

Jamari nodded, humiliated all over again.

Marcus continued.

"You wanna be ready? Then master what failed you."

For the next two weeks, that was the routine.

Same cone.

Same move.

No games. No distractions. Just reps.

While his friends posted selfies from parties and open runs, Jamari was buried in sweat and silence.

One night, Marcus tossed him a pair of beat-up ankle weights.

"Strap up."

"Seriously?" Jamari groaned.

"You wanna move faster?" Marcus asked. "Then train with something pulling you down."

Jamari didn't argue.

He just strapped up and kept it moving.

Then something started to shift.

His footwork? Cleaner.

His jumper? Quicker.

His balance? Tighter.

More than anything — his mind was clearer.

He stopped thinking about mixtapes.

Stopped comparing himself to ranked players.

He wasn't trying to impress.

He was trying to become.

One evening, Marcus sat on the bench in the garage while Jamari knocked down jumper after jumper.

No clock. No count.

Just rhythm.

"You want that run again?" Marcus asked.

Jamari paused, wiped his face with his shirt.

"Yeah," he said.

"But not to prove anything."

Marcus smirked.

"Good. Because this time, you go to compete, not convince."

Chapter 4: Same Move, Same Day

The same gym.

Same waxed floor. Same yellow lights overhead.

Same dogs running full-court with bad intentions and mean defense.

But this time, Jamari wasn't nervous.

He wasn't trying to be flashy.

He was just there to work.

Marcus stayed outside.

Didn't need to say a word.

He'd already said everything through the drills, the early mornings, and the ankle weights.

"Real players don't talk. They show up," Marcus had told him.

So Jamari showed up.

The first possession, he didn't touch the ball.

Second trip down, he set a back screen that led to a dunk.

Nobody noticed — but he did.

By the third game, he caught a swing pass on the wing, jabbed, rose up, and hit the same pull-up jumper he'd practiced a thousand times.

No celebration. No yelling.

Just the walk back on defense.

"Yo," one of the older guys said mid-game. "You was here last time, huh?"

Jamari nodded, wiping his hands on his shorts.

"You play different now."

Jamari smiled slightly.

"Been working."

"I see that."

They played for two hours.

Jamari didn't score 30.

But he made the right reads. Took the right shots. Fought over every screen.

By the time the run ended, the same players who had ignored him last time gave him dap without being asked.

"Told y'all he ain't just here for cardio," one guy joked.

Marcus didn't say anything when they walked to the car.

Until they got inside.

"Better."

Jamari looked over, waiting for more.

"Not 'cause you scored," Marcus said. "But because you finally understand what it means to work with purpose."

He paused, turning the keys in the ignition.

"That move we drilled? You didn't even think about it today, did you?"

Jamari shook his head.

"Exactly," Marcus said.

"That's what reps do.

They turn thinking into knowing.

And that's when the game slows down."

Back at home, Jamari dropped his bag at the door and walked straight to the shower. The hot water hit like victory.

He didn't need anyone to tell him he did well.

He knew.

And that was new.

Lying in bed that night, he stared at the ceiling.

He thought about every boring, painful, silent hour in the garage.

Every time he wanted to quit.

Every voice in his head that said he wasn't built for this.

And he thought…

Maybe I ain't arrived yet. But I'm getting close.

Chapter 5: Nobody Clapped

The first game of senior year was quiet.

No college scouts in the stands.

No media coverage.

Just folding chairs, parents with coffee mugs, and a ref who looked half asleep.

Jamari stretched in silence, lacing up his sneakers like he had something to prove — but not to the crowd.

To himself.

He had come too far to chase attention.

He used to care if the gym was full. If the cameras were on. If the mixtape guy was courtside.

But now?

He was locked in.

Focused on what mattered.

"Good luck," his teammate said as they walked to the court.

"I don't need luck," Jamari answered calmly. "Just the ball."

The game tipped off.

First possession, he caught the ball on the wing, jabbed, one dribble pull-up — cash.

Same move.

Same rep.

Automatic.

By halftime, he had 17 points and hadn't said a word.

The other team adjusted in the third. Double teams. Full court pressure. Trash talk.

But Jamari didn't flinch.

He didn't force.

He dissected.

Step-through. Floater. Skip pass to the corner.

Two feet in the paint, then a pivot kickout for a three.

It was surgical.

He ended the night with 28 points, 6 assists, and 3 steals — in a win.

Still, nobody clapped like they would have if his name was already in lights.

No blog posted a highlight.

No scout pulled him aside after the buzzer.

But Marcus was in the back corner of the gym.

No expression. Just watching.

After the game, Jamari approached him.

"Nothing flashy," he said.

"Exactly," Marcus replied.

"Flash fades. Fundamentals last."

Over the next few games, the numbers stacked up:

- 25 in a win
- 31 in a loss
- 18 with the flu
- 33 with a game-winner

And still — silence from colleges.

The doubters started whispering again.

"If he's that good, why don't he got offers?"

"Probably peaked already."

"He don't play on a real AAU team anyway."

One night, after dropping 30 in another empty gym, Jamari sat at the end of the bench, towel around his neck, staring at the floor.

Marcus walked up and leaned against the wall behind him.

"You frustrated?"

Jamari nodded.

"I'm doing everything right, Pops. The work. The team stuff. The wins. Still no love."

Marcus shrugged.

"You waiting on love… or legacy?"

Jamari looked up.

"Legacy don't need claps," Marcus said.

"It just needs consistency. And time."

That night, Jamari didn't post his stats.

Didn't even repost the team win.

He just went back to the gym.

One ball. One move.

Same cone.

Same drill.

Because nobody was clapping.

But he wasn't playing for noise anymore.

He was playing for something deeper.

Chapter 6: Breakthrough

The cold January air bit at Jamari's face as he stepped out of the locker room, hoodie pulled low, headphones in. Another game. Another win. Another 29 points.

Still no calls.

His coach had already emailed highlights to ten schools. Still nothing.

"They just sleeping," one teammate said.

Jamari wasn't so sure.

But he didn't let it break him.

Instead of scrolling social media, he studied film.

Instead of celebrating after games, he iced his knees and got ready for the next one.

The crowd still wasn't big.

But the whispers got louder.

"That kid on East? He different."

"He don't talk. He just work."

"Who's recruiting him?"

Nobody had an answer.

But they were all asking.

Mid-February. A regional tournament. Bigger gym. Neutral site. Coaches in the stands.

Jamari didn't change a thing.

No new move. No wild outfit. No smiles for the camera.

Just laced his shoes and locked in.

The game started fast.

The other team had a five-star guard. Ranked. Cameras followed his every move.

Jamari's job? Guard him.

He didn't say a word.

Just made him uncomfortable.

Cut off angles. Beat him to spots.

Stripped him twice. Took a charge.

Then went back down and hit a three right in his face.

By halftime, Jamari had 19.

By the fourth quarter, he had 32 and his team was up 6.

The gym got quiet.

Everyone was watching him now.

Every scout that came for the ranked guard was leaning forward.

The final buzzer sounded.

Victory.

Jamari walked off the floor without a scream.

No chest pound.

No celebration.

Just a deep breath.

Like he expected it.

Marcus was waiting by the exit, arms crossed.

"That was cute," he said, smirking.

Jamari smirked back.

"Cute?"

"Yeah. I mean, 32 is cool… but y'all only won by what? Eight?"

Jamari shook his head.

"You can't just let me have it, huh?"

Marcus shrugged.

"If I let you have it now… you might settle."

He paused.

"And I ain't train you to settle."

That night, Jamari's phone buzzed. And buzzed. And buzzed.

Three mid-majors. One HBCU. One D1 assistant asking for film.

His coach called just to say,

"Told you they were watching."

Jamari didn't scream or throw a party.

He went to the garage.

Same shoes.

Same cone.

Same drill.

Because he wasn't playing for hype.

He was becoming who they said he'd never be.

Chapter 7: The Transition

The campus looked like a movie.

Tall buildings, perfect grass, giant weight rooms, and a practice gym that felt like the pros.

Jamari had made it.

After months of silence, he finished his senior year with over a dozen offers, eventually committing to a mid-major D1 school that needed guards who could defend and stay locked in.

The coaching staff loved his mindset.

The strength coach said he had a chip on his shoulder.

Everyone smiled when he signed.

Except Marcus.

"Congratulations," he said flatly.

"Now forget everything you just did."

Jamari looked confused.

"What?"

"That high school stuff? It's gone. You just became a freshman again."

And he was right.

The first college practice was chaos.

Speed like nothing Jamari had ever seen.

Guys flying off screens, hitting shots with hands in their face.

No time to think.

Just react — or fall behind.

He missed his first three shots.

Got burned on a backdoor cut.

Coach pulled him after two minutes in the scrimmage.

"That ain't the kid I recruited," the coach snapped.

In the locker room, Jamari sat staring at his shoes.

Everything felt heavy. Too fast. Too much.

He called Marcus that night.

"I don't know, man," he said. "It's like… I ain't ready."

There was a long pause on the line.

"You thought this was the end of the journey?" Marcus asked.

"Boy… this ain't the end. It's the start of the next grind."

"You want to be respected? Then re-earn it. Here. Now."

So he did.

While others scrolled through Instagram, he watched film.

While teammates joked in the locker room, he was in the training room stretching and getting shots up.

He showed up 45 minutes early to practice.

Stayed late.

Didn't ask for attention.

Didn't expect minutes.

He just worked.

Weeks passed. Then months.

By the time Christmas break hit, Jamari wasn't just surviving practice — he was thriving in it.

He'd earned the respect of the assistant coaches.

His name started getting called more in huddles.

He even got a few garbage-time minutes in games — and made the most of them.

One day after practice, the head coach pulled him aside.

"We didn't know what we really had when we got you," he said.

"But we're starting to see it now."

Jamari nodded, breathing heavy.

"I'm still just getting started."

That night, he walked outside into the cold winter air.

He looked up at the sky and smiled.

Not because he was there…

But because he still wasn't done.

Chapter 8: Setback Season

Midway through the season, things were finally clicking.

Jamari wasn't starting — not yet — but he'd carved out minutes.

Defensive stops. Smart passes. Steady presence.

He didn't need the spotlight.

He just wanted to stay in the rotation.

Then it happened.

A drive.

A step.

A loud pop.

He hit the ground hard, grabbing his ankle before the pain even registered.

Trainers rushed over.

Teammates circled, looking down.

Coach knelt beside him, whispering,

"We'll get you right."

But Jamari didn't hear it.

All he could hear was doubt.

Not now. Not again.

Grade 2 ankle sprain.

Four to six weeks.

Not career-ending.

But just long enough to feel like the game was moving on without him.

The gym became torture.

He still showed up to practice.

Watched film. Sat on the sideline in slides with a boot on.

He clapped. Supported. Acted okay.

But deep down?

He felt forgotten.

Late one night, Jamari sat alone in the dorm hallway, hoodie up, scrolling through clips of other guards shining — the ones taking his minutes.

He wanted to throw the phone.

Wanted to scream.

Instead, he called the one man who never sugarcoated anything.

"I don't get it," Jamari said into the phone. "I was finally getting my shot."

"So now what?" Marcus said.

"You done?"

Jamari sighed.

"Man, you know I ain't done. I just feel… stuck."

"Good," Marcus replied. "That means you're still fighting. You only feel stuck when you're trying to move forward."

Jamari didn't respond.

So Marcus hit him with it straight.

"Use this time. Watch everything. Learn tendencies. Study. Get mentally dangerous."

"And when you come back… you won't just be ready to play — you'll be ready to lead."

And Jamari listened.

For the next four weeks, he wasn't just healing — he was preparing.

He tracked plays. Noted opponents' weak hands.

Watched film with a notepad.

Asked questions during huddles.

His mind sharpened like a blade.

By the time he returned, his body was stronger and his game was smoother.

But the difference?

His IQ.

He didn't just react anymore — he anticipated.

That first day back at practice, he made a no-look dime that had the team buzzing.

Coach raised an eyebrow.

"Where's this been hiding?"

Jamari wiped sweat from his face.

"It wasn't hiding. I was just waiting to come back smarter."

He still wasn't the star.

But he was turning into something better:

A player that coaches trusted.

Chapter 9: Earned, Not Given

By the time conference play rolled around, Jamari wasn't just back—

he was noticed.

No longer the quiet freshman in the corner,

he'd become the first guard off the bench.

Some nights, he logged twenty-plus minutes.

Other nights, he finished the game on the floor.

And every time he checked in, it wasn't just to fill space—

it was to make an impact.

Screens? He called them out before they came.

Rotations? Crisp. Predictable. Solid.

And on offense, he wasn't flashy—

he was effective.

The kind of player that made everyone else better.

But it didn't come without friction.

In a road game against their top rival,

the starting point guard, Zeke, was struggling—

turnovers, missed reads, sloppy energy.

Coach glanced down the bench.

"Jamari."

He checked in with three minutes left in a tie game.

Crowd roaring.

ESPN cameras rolling.

And with one timeout left, everything on the line—

Jamari walked the ball up slow, like he'd done it a thousand times.

First possession: dish to the wing, relocate, get it back, swing again—

the ball moved, the defense shifted,

and they scored.

Second possession: he caught the hedge early,

split the double, and dropped a bounce pass through traffic for a layup.

The bench exploded.

Zeke, sitting just a few feet away, didn't clap.

After the win, while the team celebrated, Jamari pulled Zeke aside.

"I'm not trying to take your spot," he said.

"I'm trying to win."

Zeke didn't say much. Just nodded.

But respect was earned that night.

From there, Jamari's role grew.

Not just minutes.

Responsibility.

He became the unofficial leader of the scout team—

calling out coverages, holding guys accountable.

He even gave a halftime speech during a sluggish outing.

"You waiting on someone to save the game?" he asked, staring around the locker room.

"Or are you ready to be that someone?"

It wasn't rehearsed.

It was real.

And they responded.

Back in his dorm, Jamari kept the same routines.

Still watched film.

Still hit the training room early.

Still texted Marcus after games—even the good ones.

"Proud," Marcus would reply. "But stay hungry."

Because for Jamari, it was never about arriving.

It was about becoming.

And somewhere between the ice baths, the missed calls home,

and the long nights of doubt that once haunted him—

Jamari realized something powerful:

He didn't need to be the best.

He just needed to be ready when it mattered.

And now?

He was ready for anything.

Chapter 10: He Ain't Just Good

The crowd roared.

Cameras flashed.

Announcers mispronounced his last name.

Scouts scribbled notes.

Jamari stood at midcourt, locked in. Calm.

He was playing in his first college conference championship.

From a kid nobody recruited, to the player everybody had to gameplan for.

But he didn't need the moment to be loud.

He already heard everything he needed — in his mind.

Marcus's voice.

"Good gets noticed.

Great gets remembered."

That line had haunted Jamari for years.

But now… it made sense.

He wasn't trying to be flashy anymore.

Didn't need mixtapes or rankings or hype.

What he built didn't show up on social media.

It showed up in the fourth quarter.

In his poise.

His pace.

His precision.

He wasn't a star.

He was a solution.

The game tipped off.

Jamari didn't force anything.

He just played his game.

- A charge taken.
- A corner three knocked down.
- A pocket pass off a ball screen.
- A closeout that forced a bad shot.

Nothing sexy.

But everything winning.

They lost by three.

It hurt.

But not like it would've years ago.

Not because it didn't matter…

But because Jamari knew he left it all out there.

And something deeper hit him that night:

The goal was never to be perfect. It was to be prepared.

After the game, a reporter found him in the tunnel.

"You played a hell of a game," she said.

"What do you think separates you from other guards in your position?"

Jamari thought about it.

Then smiled.

"They play for claps.

I play for keeps."

She looked surprised.

"And what would you say to the kids coming up, the ones who don't have rankings, hype, or offers?"

Jamari looked right into the camera lens.

"I was you."

"But let me tell you something…

You don't need a crowd to build greatness.

You just need discipline, silence, and the will to keep going when nobody claps."

That night, Jamari walked out of the arena and saw Marcus waiting by the car.

Same stance. Same look. Same arms crossed.

"So," Marcus asked, "how many you leave out there tonight?"

Jamari smirked.

"None."

Marcus nodded once.

That was all he ever needed.

Final Lines:

He wasn't born with it.

- He wasn't handed it.

He built it.

Brick by brick. Rep by rep. Doubt by doubt.

He started out chasing greatness.

Now?

He walked in it.

He ain't just good.

He's built for whatever comes next.

Made in the USA
Coppell, TX
02 July 2025

51275829R00018